Do You Like Experimenting with STEM?

Diane Lindsey Reeves

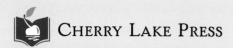

CHERRY LAKE PRESS

Published in the United States of America by Cherry Lake Publishing Group
Ann Arbor, Michigan
www.cherrylakepublishing.com

Reading Adviser: Beth Walker Gambro, MS, Ed., Reading Consultant, Yorkville, IL

Photo Credits: cover, page 10: © marvent/Shutterstock; page 5: © JohnnyVillan/iStock; page 6: © Daisy Daisy/ Shutterstock; page 7: © Nong2/Shutterstock; pages 8, 13: © Dragon Images/Shutterstock; page 9: © CrizzyStudio/ Shutterstock; page 11: © Elnur/Shutterstock; pages 12, 18, 25: © DC Studio/Shutterstock; page 14: © kosmos111/ Shutterstock; page 15: © APChanel/Shutterstock; page 16: © Edw/Shutterstock; page 17: © felipe caparros/ Shutterstock; pages 19, 30: © Gorodenkoff/Shutterstock; page 20: NASA; page 21: © PeopleImages.com - Yuri A/ Shutterstock; page 22: © baranq/Shutterstock; page 23: © Prathankarnpap/Shutterstock; page 24: © Inside Creative House/Shutterstock; page 26: © zstock/Shutterstock; page 27: © sirtravelalot/Shutterstock; page 31: © Fernando Avendano/Shutterstock

Cherry Lake Press is an imprint of Cherry Lake Publishing Group.

Library of Congress Cataloging-in-Publication Data has been filed and is available at catalog.loc.gov

Cherry Lake Publishing Group would like to acknowledge the work of the Partnership for 21st Century Learning, a Network of Battelle for Kids. Please visit *http://www.battelleforkids.org/networks/p21* for more information.

Printed in the United States of America
Corporate Graphics

Diane Lindsey Reeves likes to write books that help students figure out what they want to be when they grow up. She mostly lives in Washington, D.C., but spends as much time as she can in North Carolina and South Carolina with her grandkids.

CONTENTS

Experiment with STEM Careers

Figuring out what you want to be when you grow up can be tricky. There are so many choices! How are you supposed to know which one to pick? Here's an idea... follow the clues!

The fact that you are reading a book called *Do You Like Experimenting with STEM?* is your first clue. It suggests that you have an interest in science, technology, engineering, and math. True? If so, this is the right book for you! Your **interests** say a lot about who you are and what makes you tick. What do you like doing best?

Abilities are things that you are naturally good at doing. Another word for ability is talent. Everyone has natural talents and abilities. Some are more obvious than others. What are you really good at doing?

Curiosity offers up other career clues. To succeed in any career, you have to learn what it takes to do that job. You may have to go to college or trade school. It may take gaining new skills and getting experience. Curiosity about a subject keeps you at it until you are an expert. What do you want to know more about?

Interests. Abilities. Curiosity. These clues can help you find a career that's right for you.

FIND THE CLUES!

Each chapter includes several clues about careers you might enjoy.

INTERESTS: **What do you like doing?**

ABILITIES: **What are you good at doing?**

CURIOSITY: **What do you want to learn more about?**

Are You a Future STEM Whiz?

WOULD YOU ENJOY...

Exploring a math career you've never heard of?
(see page 8)

Helping save the world if another pandemic hits?
(see page 10)

Using data to solve business problems? (see page 12)

Making the earth a greener place? (see page 14)

Solving crimes with science? (see page 16)

Protecting computer systems from cyberattacks?
(see page 18)

Working with numbers in ways that count? (see page 20)

Designing cool new apps for smartphones? (see page 22)

Helping sick people get better? (see page 24)

**Making good use of alternative fuels—one house at
a time?** (see page 26)

READ ON FOR MORE CLUES ABOUT STEM CAREERS!

Actuary

A person who helps organizations plan for the future and protect against loss.

You might not know what an actuary does. Lots of people don't. But chances are their work affects you in one way or another. They use math, **statistics**, and business skills to figure out **risk**. As in, the risk that a house at the beach will get damaged by a hurricane. Or the risk that a sports star will get injured in a game. They use this information to insure people and organizations from the risk. That way, if a hurricane hits, there is insurance to repair the house. This job is often spotted on best careers lists.

CLUES!

INTEREST: Keeping track of sports statistics

ABILITY: Solving problems

CURIOSITY: Using math to help people

INVESTIGATE!

NOW: Run for class treasurer in your class or school.

LATER: Earn a college degree in math, economics, or actuarial science.

Biochemist

A person who studies chemical processes in living things.

Biochemists came to the rescue during the **COVID-19 pandemic**. The race was on to find vaccines and cures for the awful virus. Biochemists researched how different medicines affected the human body. They came up with solutions in record time! This type of research is called applied research. It is when biochemists use research to solve a specific problem. Biochemists also do basic research. This is when they want to learn more about something like **DNA**. Many biochemists work with medicines. Others work with food, technology, or cosmetics.

CLUES!

INTEREST: Experimenting with a chemistry set

ABILITY: Wrestling with a good science hypothesis

CURIOSITY: What happens when you mix biology and chemistry

INVESTIGATE!

NOW: Join the STEM club at school.

LATER: Earn a college degree or degrees in biology, chemistry, or biochemistry.

Data Scientist

A person who interprets data to help businesses make decisions.

Data scientists start with a huge mess of information, or **data**. They use technology to sort and organize data in useful ways. Their goal is to answer questions and spot trends. They use data to improve how a business works and what it does. A big part of their job is to **analyze** data. That means they look for order and patterns in the data. Data scientists have to know a lot about math, technology, and business. Data provides a gold mine of information when someone knows where to look.

CLUES!

INTEREST: All things high-tech

ABILITY: Figuring out answers to tough questions

CURIOSITY: Keeping up with trends

INVESTIGATE!

NOW: Learn a new computer programming language.

LATER: Earn a college degree in data science.

Environmental Engineer

A person who works to prevent, control, or repair environmental problems.

Environmental engineers work on some of the world's biggest problems. This includes things like climate change. It also means providing access to food and clean water supplies. Making the world a safer, greener place is a goal they share. Sometimes they work to fix things that are already causing problems, like pollution. Other times they try to find new solutions. These include things like energy and **alternative fuels**. They all use creative math and science skills to get the job done.

CLUES!

INTEREST: Enjoying the great outdoors

ABILITY: Getting good grades in math and science classes

CURIOSITY: Creating a **sustainable** world

INVESTIGATE!

NOW: Get involved in local Earth Day activities.

LATER: Earn a college degree in civil or environmental engineering.

Forensic Science Technician

A person who collects evidence at crime scenes.

Forensic science technicians investigate crime scenes. Their job is to collect clues to find out who committed the crime. Technicians take photographs and make sketches of the obvious clues. Then they carefully collect evidence like fingerprints and blood samples. It's important that they don't miss a thing. Sometimes something as small as a strand of hair helps crack the case. Technicians take all the evidence back to a laboratory. That is where they run tests. Many times, DNA or fingerprints help identify suspects.

CLUES!

INTEREST: Crime shows on TV

ABILITY: Paying attention to detail

CURIOSITY: Proving that crime doesn't pay

INVESTIGATE!

NOW: Go online to find out how to collect fingerprints.

LATER: Earn a college degree in natural or forensic science.

Information Security Analyst

A person who protects computer networks from cyberattacks.

Hackers beware! An information security, or infosec, analyst is trying to outsmart you. Their job is to keep business and government computer systems safe from intruders. Cyberattacks aren't only a nuisance. They can also be dangerous. Computer systems run everything from banks and hospitals to energy supplies and airports. If someone disrupts these systems, bad things can happen. That's why infosec analysts constantly watch computer networks for security problems. They install security programs to protect computer systems. When all else fails, they investigate security break-ins and cybercrimes.

CLUES!

INTEREST: Reading a good mystery

ABILITY: Figuring out whodunnit

CURIOSITY: How computers work

INVESTIGATE!

NOW: Find out more about safe online surfing at https://sos.fbi.gov.

LATER: Earn a computer degree or get special training at IT boot camps.

Mathematician

A person who uses math to solve problems in business, government, and technology.

Mathematician is a career that really adds up! Mathematicians are curious problem-solvers. They use numbers to find answers for business questions. For example, "What is the best way to provide flights to 150 cities using 32 jets?" They use numbers to solve questions about science, like "What are the math codes found in DNA?" They also answer questions about engineering, medicine, and technology. They work in all kinds of places. You might find them working at stock exchanges, government agencies, banks, or insurance companies. Mathematicians seem to find a lot of job satisfaction. This career often shows up on best career lists.

CLUES!

INTEREST: Solving complicated math problems in your head

ABILITY: Mastering tough math classes

CURIOSITY: How numbers work

INVESTIGATE!

NOW: Take as many math classes as you can.

LATER: Earn a college degree in mathematics.

Mobile App Developer

A person who creates, programs, and tests applications for mobile devices.

People are glued to their smartphones these days. It seems like you can do just about anything on a smartphone. Deposit a check? Play a fun game? Learn a new language? Read a book? Find your way home? Yes, there are mobile apps for all that and more. And it's all thanks to mobile app developers. The job requires an impressive mix of creative talent and technical skill. App developers use computer programming skills to create apps that people can't stop using.

CLUES!

INTEREST: Playing games on your favorite device

ABILITY: Writing computer code

CURIOSITY: How to make even cooler mobile apps

INVESTIGATE!

NOW: Make a list of mobile apps you want to create someday.

LATER: Get a college degree and/or certification in computer science or mobile app development.

Physician Assistant (PA)

A person who provides patient health care.

Physician assistants (PAs) do a lot of the same things that doctors do. They diagnose diseases, treat patients, and prescribe medicines. They work in doctor's offices, clinics, and hospitals. There are three differences. One is that PAs cannot perform surgery. Another is that PAs must be supervised by a doctor. The big difference is that they don't need 10 to 14 years of training like doctors do. PAs need a bachelor's degree, health care experience, and a 2-year master's degree. There is a huge need for PAs to take care of the world's growing and aging populations.

CLUES!

INTERESTS: Weird diseases and strange ailments

ABILITIES: Taking care of people and pets

CURIOSITY: How the human body works

INVESTIGATE!

NOW: Take a first aid course at your local community center.

LATER: Earn a master's degree in a PA program.

Solar Installer

A person who installs photovoltaic (PV) systems that convert sunlight into energy

It's one thing to talk about using smarter energy sources. It's another thing to do something about it. Solar installers work in the solar industry to make change happen. They work with clients to plan the best system for their needs. Then the job gets hands-on. They put the system together and install it. Then they connect the PV panels to an electrical source. The big bonus for solar customers? Sunlight is free. Customers save a lot of money on utility bills. Of course, sunlight beams down from the sky. That means that much of a solar installer's work is done on rooftops.

CLUES!

INTERESTS: Helping save Earth

ABILITIES: Working with your hands

CURIOSITY: How solar energy works

INVESTIGATE!

NOW: Look online to find instructions on how to make your own solar oven.

LATER: Get on-the-job training.

STEM Workshop

Keep investigating those career clues until you find a career that's right for you! Here are more ways to explore.

Join a Club

Find out if your school has a STEM club. If not, ask a favorite STEM teacher to sponsor one.

Talk to People with Interesting Careers

Ask your teacher or parent to help you connect with someone who has a career like the one you want. Be ready to ask lots of questions!

Volunteer

Help organize your school's science fair or STEM day.

Attend Career Day

School career days can be a great way to find out more about different careers. Make the most of this opportunity.

Explore Online

With adult supervision, use your favorite search engine to look online for information about careers you are interested in.

Participate in Take Your Daughters and Sons to Work Day

Every year on the fourth Thursday of April, kids all over the world go to work with their parents or other trusted adults to find out what the world of work is really like.

Find out more at: https://daughtersandsonstowork.org

Resources

Actuary
Be an Actuary
https://www.beanactuary.org

Biochemist
Chem 4 Kids
http://www.chem4kids.com

Data Scientist
Code.org
https://studio.code.org/courses

Environmental Engineer
Time for Kids: Environment
https://www.timeforkids.com/g56/sections/environment

Forensic Science Technician
Forensics for Kids
Ross, Melissa. *Forensics for Kids: The Science and History of Crime Solving.* Chicago, IL: Chicago Review Press, 2022.

Mathematician
Math Game Time
https://www.mathgametime.com

Mobile App Developer
Scratch
https://scratch.mit.edu

Physician Assistant
Wilsdon, Christina, Patricia Daniels, and Jen Agresta. *Ultimate Body-pedia.* Washington, DC: National Geographic Kids, 2014.

Security Information Analyst
Cybersmart Challenge
https://www.esafety.gov.au/educators/classroom-resources/ cybersmart-challenge/student-home

Solar Photovoltaic Installer
Bill Nye—How Stuff Works: Solar Power
https://www.youtube.com/watch?v=av24fEMhDoU

Glossary

abilities (uh-BIH-luh-teez) natural talents or acquired skills

alternative fuels (ahl-TUHR-nuh-tiv FYOOLZ) fuels other than gasoline for powering vehicles

analyze (AH-nuh-lyz) study something carefully to understand it

COVID-19 (KOH-vid-nyn-teen) coronavirus; an infectious disease that spread throughout the world starting in 2019

curiosity (kyur-ee-AH-suh-tee) strong desire to know or learn about something

cyberattack (SY-buhr-uh-tak) attempt by hackers to damage or destroy a computer network or system

data (DAY-tuh) information used to form opinions or solve problems

DNA (DEE EN AY) the molecule that carries our genes

hacker (HAA-kuhr) someone who has special skills for getting into computer systems without permission

interests (IN-tuh-ruhsts) things or activities that a person enjoys or is concerned about

pandemic (pan-DEH-mik) outbreak of a disease that affects the whole world.

photovoltaic (foh-toh-vahl-TAY-ik) conversion of light into electricity using semiconducting materials

risk (RIHSK) possibility of loss, harm, or danger.

statistics (stuh-TIH-stiks) process of collecting and classifying data to draw conclusions about it

sustainable (suh-STAY-nuh-buhl) done in a way that does not use up natural resources

Index